D0408704

Pooped Puppies

RONNIE
SELLERS
PRODUCTIONS
-Gift Books-
PORTLAND, MAINE

Published by Ronnie Sellers Productions, Inc.

P.O. Box 818, Portland, Maine 04104
For ordering information:
Phone: 1-800-MAKE-FUN (800-625-3386)
Fax: (207) 772-6814
Visit our Web site: www.makefun.com
E-mail: rsp@rsvp.com

Series Editor: Robin Haywood
Photo Editors: Mary Baldwin, Amanda Mooney,
Jennifer O'Toole
Designer: Mary Baldwin, Patti Urban

ISBN: 1-56906-575-6

Printed and bound in China.
Cover image © LEDA, Inc.

Pooped Puppies

Life's too short to work like a dog

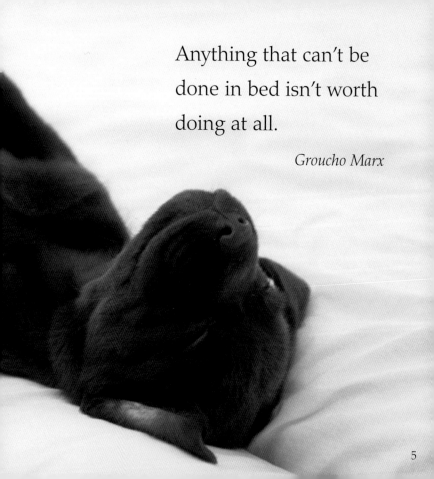

Anything that can't be
done in bed isn't worth
doing at all.

Groucho Marx

5

... slip from workaholic to bum real easy.

Matthew Broderick

Work is not always required.
There is such a thing as
sacred idleness.

George MacDonald

We need quiet time
to examine our lives
openly and honestly
. . . spending quiet
time alone gives your
mind an opportunity
to renew itself and
create order.

Susan L. Taylor

11

Naps are nature's
way of reminding
you that life is nice
— like a beautiful,
softly swinging
hammock strung
between birth
and infinity.

Peggy Noonan

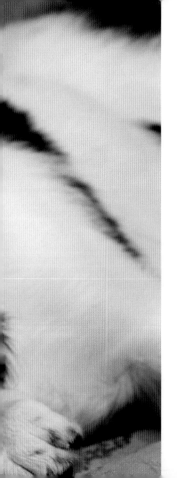

Sundays; quiet islands on the tossing seas of life.

S. W. Duffield

Blessed is the person
who is too busy to
worry in the daytime
and too sleepy to
worry at night.

Author unknown

In a dream you are never eighty.

Anne Sexton

I have long been of the opinion that if work were such a splendid thing the rich would have kept more of it for themselves.

Bruce Grocott

21

I don't generally feel anything until noon; then it's time for my nap.

Bob Hope

Tension is who you
think you should be.
Relaxation is who
you are.

Chinese proverb

Think what a better world it would be if we all, the whole world, had milk and cookies about three o'clock every afternoon and then lay down on our blankets for a nap.

Barbara Jordan

Fatigue is the best pillow.

Benjamin Franklin

Besides the noble art of getting things done, there is a nobler art of leaving things undone. The wisdom of life consists in the elimination of nonessentials.

Lin Yutang

Anything worth doing
is worth doing slowly.

Mae West

If you can dream it,
you can do it.

Walt Disney

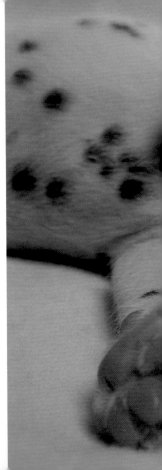

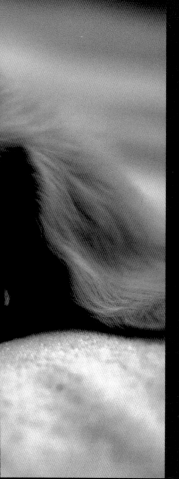

Whatever you can
do or dream, you
can begin it.
Boldness has
genius, power
and magic in it.

Johann Wolfgang von Goethe

Sleeping is no mean art: for its sake one must stay awake all day.

Friedrich Nietzsche

Work is the refuge
of those who have
nothing better to do.

Oscar Wilde

Embrace simplicity,
Reduce selfishness,
Have few desires.

Lao-tzu

Nothing cures
insomnia like the
realization that it's
time to get up.

Author unknown

Learning to ignore things
is one of the great paths
to inner peace.

Robert J. Sawyer

47

Simple pleasures are the last refuge of the complex.

Oscar Wilde

Sometimes the most important thing in a whole day is the rest we take between two deep breaths.

Etty Hillesum

51

52

The more faithfully
you listen to the voices
within you, the better
you will hear what is
sounding outside.

Dag Hammarskjold

Climb the mountains and get their good tidings. Nature's peace will flow into you as sunshine flows into trees. The winds will blow their own freshness into you, and the storms their energy, while cares will drop off like autumn leaves.

John Muir

Dreams are illustrations . . .
from the book your soul is
writing about you.

Marsha Norman

To sit with a dog on a hillside on a glorious afternoon is to be back in Eden, where doing nothing was not boring — it was peace.

Milan Kundera

I've developed a new philosophy . . .
I only dread one day at a time.

Charlie Brown (Charles Schulz)

Peace is rarely denied
to the peaceful.

Johann von Schiller

63

The reason why
worry kills more
people than work
is that more people
worry than work.

Robert Frost

Consciousness:

that annoying time

between naps.

Author unknown

Problems always
look smaller after
a warm meal and a
good night's sleep.

Anonymous

So little time,

and so little to do.

Oscar Levant

I don't have anything against work. I just figure, why deprive somebody who really loves it.

Dobie Gillis

Dreaming permits each and every one of us to be quietly and safely insane every night of our lives.

Charles William Dement

I love sleep. My life has the tendency to fall apart when I'm awake, you know?

Ernest Hemingway

If you are losing your leisure, look out, you may be losing your soul.

Anonymous

No day is so bad it can't
be fixed with a nap.

Carrie Snow

We spend most of our time and energy in a kind of horizontal thinking. We move along the surface of things . . . but, there are times when we must stop. We sit still. We lose ourselves in a pile of leaves or in its memory. We listen, and breezes from a whole other world begin to whisper.

James Carroll

83

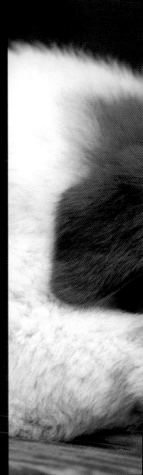

Sometimes opportunity
knocks, but most of the
time it sneaks up and
then quietly steals away.

Doug Larson

I try to take one day at a time, but sometimes several days attack me at once.

Jennifer Yane

The mark of a successful
person is one who has
spent an entire day
on the bank of a river
without feeling guilty
about it.

Author unknown

How beautiful it is to
do nothing, and then
to rest afterward.

Spanish proverb

If people
concentrated
on the really
important things
in life, there'd be
a shortage of
fishing poles.

Doug Larson

If your dreams turn
to dust . . . vacuum.

Author unknown

A good rest is half the work.

Yugoslav proverb

Sitting quietly,
doing nothing,
spring comes and
the grass grows
by itself.

Zen proverb

Troubles are a lot like people — they grow bigger if you nurse them.

Author unknown

Sometimes it's important
to work for that pot of
gold. But other times it's
essential to take time off
and to make sure that your
most important decision in
the day simply consists of
choosing which color of
the rainbow to slide down.

Douglas Pagels

Life is something that
happens when you can't
get to sleep.

Fran Lebowitz

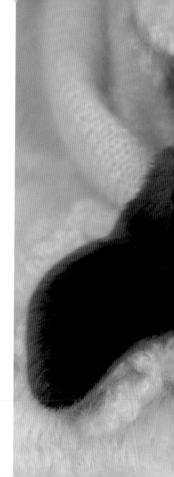

Hold fast to dreams.
For if dreams die, life
is a broken-winged
bird that cannot fly.

James Langston Hughes

I like work; it fascinates me. I can sit and look at it for hours.

Jerome K. Jerome

Credits